Margaret Stewart Barbour Simpson

The Scottish Songstress, Caroline Baroness Nairne

Margaret Stewart Barbour Simpson

The Scottish Songstress, Caroline Baroness Nairne

ISBN/EAN: 9783337008284

Printed in Europe, USA, Canada, Australia, Japan

Cover: Foto ©ninafisch / pixelio.de

More available books at **www.hansebooks.com**

LADY NAIRNE AND HER SON

THE

SCOTTISH SONGSTRESS

CAROLINE BARONESS NAIRNE

BY

HER GREAT GRAND-NIECE

EDINBURGH & LONDON
OLIPHANT ANDERSON & FERRIER
1894

LIST OF ILLUSTRATIONS

THE SCOTTISH SONGSTRESS

CAROLINE BARONESS NAIRNE

———·+·———

WHO can tell the power of music and of song? Although the essence of time, they transcend time. As the wind or as the sunshine, their influence is everywhere, yet undefined. It may be like a breeze or a storm, a stray ray or the meridian glory. It is all around us. We are but the losers if our capacity be small. Oliver Wendell Holmes calls music a "bath for the soul." Shall we call it a tideless sea, or an atmosphere of light? For those who love solidity, music is like a temple or a shrine where the greatest in all ages have laid their offering, or at least inscribed their names, ere they passed on into

what is darkness to us and purer light to them.
But though the singers pass on, what they
were at their best remains in their song.   The
mother sings the lullaby at the cradle; the
"toddlin' wean" runs an errand to the nearest
shop, humming it as it goes; and thus a stream
of song is set aflowing.

We had grown up so loving and learning
Lady Nairne's songs, that it was a special joy
to stand, in the summer of 1893, near the spot,
at once her birthplace and her grave, where, as
another poet wrote, "Lady Nairne had walked
and ridden, and loved and sung, till Strathearn,
that made Caroline Oliphant so beautiful and
such a poet, was made by her more lovely
and lyric still."   It was nearly fifty years by
the calendar since the day that her eyes were
closed to all that lovely land.   Fifty years!

Carmina morte carent

CAROLINA OLIPHANT

BARONESS NAIRNE

Born at Gask, 1766

Died at Gask, 1845

So the inscription stands on her obelisk,
and the full, rich nature-life all around on that
glorious summer day spoke of immortality for
her as for her verse. We could think of how
her life grew,—from the day she was named
Caroline in honour of the exiled Prince Charles,
—through the pretty " Miss Car " of the school-
room, till she blossomed into the " Flower of
Strathearn "; and, better still, how her mind
grew in her songs. " The auld pear tree" is
there, and to her, as to it, a ring of age meant
a year of growth. There is the winding Earn,
the auld house, the auld dial; but the sweet
singer is awa'! The subject of her song, more
beautiful than ever, framed in the setting of this
glorious summer, lives on ; and she lies sleeping.

> "Oh, the auld house, the auld house,
>   What tho' the rooms were wee !
> Oh ! kind hearts were dwelling there,
>   And bairnies fu' o' glee ;
> The wild rose and the jessamine
>   Still hang upon the wa' ;
> How mony cherish'd memories
>   Do they, sweet flowers, reca' !

Still flourishing the auld pear tree
   The bairnies liked to see,
And oh, how often did they speir
   When ripe they a' wad be !

Drawn by Lady Nairne

The voices sweet, the wee bit feet
   Aye rinnin' here and there,
The merry shout Oh ! whiles we greet
   To think we'll hear nae mair !

The setting sun, the setting sun,
  How glorious it gaed doon!
The cloudy splendour raised our hearts
  To cloudless skies aboon!
The auld dial, the auld dial,
  It tauld how time did pass;
The wintry winds hae dung it doon,
  Now hid 'mang weeds and grass."

We have seen on French roads larger and
lesser milestones, divisions and subdivisions;
so the fiftieth year seems like one of those
larger milestones, a time to stop in this fast
age of ours, and look at the writer of these
songs from this distance, with the lights and
shadows of well-nigh half a century.

"Why is it that we never, never know
  The beauty of our treasures while they're ours?
A little way removed must be the flower
From where we breathe its perfume, ere we can
See all its beauteous bloom and paint it so.
A stone's cast from us must the sheltering tree
Rise in its greenness, ere we can behold
Its perfect form against the hill or sky.
Too interwoven with our own heart strings,
Too much a unison with our life's song,
Is all that meets us in the object loved
That we should well describe it. "

In a friend's house, when we got tired of the immediate surroundings, we looked through a telescope and read the lettering on the pier-head of the opposite coast. Shall we do so now ere the shore recedes further, looking at the outline of Lady Nairne's chequered life till she returned to Gask to die?

"*Buried among his works.*" So the Danish guide said of Thorwaldsen's grave at Copenhagen. All round the courtyard were the galleries, divided into little rooms, each containing a masterpiece, and he lay under a simple mound of ivy, with the words, " Bertel Thorwaldsen." No monument marked his grave. His works were his monument. *Her* monument is surely the songs she sang ; and we say of her, " Buried among her works"— not of sculpture, but of song.

The visit to the spot recalled many memories. As we wandered on the turf, we thought of those who had gone since we last stood there. The proprietor of the mansion, the sweet songstress, the grandniece who made us sing the songs, and the brother whose ringing voice had blended its notes with ours, had all met above! We returned at night to the lovely villa on the Tay where our grandmother, Lady Nairne's niece, had told us many histories of her young days. We sometimes fear that the gentle art of story telling is dying out, or disappearing like the old hostelries on our deserted highroads. Long journeys by stage-coach and the more expensive postage of letters and absence of post-cards made stories a more essential part of the life in olden times; and the gloamin' in Scotland, when it was more difficult to get the lights lit, when there were tinder-box and flint and steel instead of matches, favoured their growth. At anyrate, our grandmother used to make the moments fly with her tales of bygone days.

Lady Nairne had watched her sister, Mrs. Stewart, my grandmother's mother, pass away. After the oil-painting of Bonskeid had been placed opposite her bed, our grandmother, then a schoolgirl, was eagerly expected. "Take the storeroom key and have it brightened," she said to her little maid Christie;[1] "Miss Stewart must find it in good order." Lady Nairne used to say, "Ask me no questions about the visible glory that seemed to encircle my beloved sister in that solemn hour." Another story flits across our minds as we write, like a shadow on the wall. It must have been intended for an older listener, for we thought it pretty, but did not take in the meaning. A girl was in doubt as to whether she should accept or refuse a lover. "Gang and listen to what the kirk bells say," was the shrewd advice. "Well, what do they say?" the girl was asked when she came back. "The bells said, 'Tak' him, Jenny; tak' him, Jenny!'" These and many of the Gask stories were told in a bow window

---

[1] She still survives at the age of ninety-seven, and lives not far from the South Inch in Perth, where she delights to tell these old histories.

overlooking the Tay, with the Grampians beyond.

There is now a railway along the whole road between Springland and Bonskeid, the two homes of our childhood; but when we were young we used to leave the train at Dunkeld, near where the Wolf of Badenoch (whose descendant had married Lady Nairne's eldest sister) lies buried, and enter the stage-coach close by the lovely grounds of Murthly Castle, belonging to the Stewart line. It was in these grounds that Lady Nairne passed through the crisis of her life. " She was on a visit," my mother has told us, "to the old Castle of Murthly, where an English clergyman had also arrived. He was a winner of souls. At morning worship she was in her place with the household, and listened to what God's ambassador said on the promise, ' Him that cometh unto Me, I will in no wise cast out.' Faith grasped it. From that hour she never had one doubt of God's love to her in Christ.

But that forenoon she was seen no more. Her fair face was spoiled with weeping when she again appeared. Her eye had caught the glory of the Son of God, and burned with love to Him of whom she henceforth could say, 'Whose I am and whom I serve.'"

When not beside the Tay, it was within sound of the rushing Tummel, in the very heart of Perthshire, that we eagerly listened to our mother's tales. Hers was a magician's wand. The land she led us into was an enchanted country. The scenery around helped the artist story-teller. When reduced to paper the tales may seem dull and cold, like lantern-slides without the magic light. Later years tell us that it is not so much the stories themselves as the listeners which make these old tales live. Life for us older people puts in the punctuation, even the pronunciation, but to a child the web is woven quicker than we can supply the flax. Our fancy loves to linger over the long summer days, where the country

around reminded my mother of the happy
summers spent on the Continent as a girl of
fifteen with her grand-aunt, Lady Nairne.
The bound volume of that loved singer's *Lays
from Strathearn* was never far away. It
seemed to illustrate the country round. The
rowan tree, watched by day at one end of
the Bonskeid bowling-green, with its crimson
berries and its golden leaves, was sung of at
night with childish ardour.

"O! Rowan tree, O! Rowan tree, thou'lt aye be dear to me
Intwin'd thou art wi' mony ties o' hame and infancy.
Thy leaves were aye the first o' spring, thy flow'rs the
    simmer's pride ;
There was nae sic a bonny tree, in a' the countrie side.
            O! Rowan tree.

How fair wert thou in simmer time, wi' a' thy clusters
    white !
How rich and gay thy autumn dress, wi' berries red and
    bright !
On thy fair stem were mony names, which now nae mair
    I see,
But they're engraven on my heart — forgot they ne'er
    can be !
            O! Rowan tree."

In the same way, the bonnie burn beyond was at night arrested in its course and captured in song.

> "Bonnie ran the burnie doon,
>   Wand'rin' and windin';
> Sweetly sang the birds aboon,
>   Care never mindin'.
>
> The gentle simmer wind
>   Was their nursie saft and kind,
> And it rockit them, and rockit them,
>   All in their bowers sae hie.
>
> The mossy rock was there,
>   And the water-lily fair,
> And the little trout would sport aboot
>   All in the sunny beam."

If a Highland piper appeared on the gravel, it was easy to make him into a hundred. A child loves multiplication, subtraction to it is not so easy. And the voices pealed out the melody—

> "Wi' a hundred pipers an' a', an a',
> Wi' a hundred pipers an' a', an' a';
> We'll up an' gie them a blaw, a blaw,
> Wi' a hundred pipers an' a', an' a'."

If a stray lamb wandered past, we had its

picture in her grand-aunt's lines, which my
mother loved to repeat—

"The mitherless lammie ne'er miss'd its ain mammie,
  We tentit it kindly by nicht and by day;
The bairnies made game o't, it had a blythe hame o't,
  Its food was the gowan, wi' dewdrops o' May."

It was her own vivid imagination that made
those evenings so delightful. She used to say
when no longer able to travel: "Send me a
telegram, that I may fancy it all. Even in my
strong days imaginations of a place were sometimes better to me than the reality." If we
were beside her putting up a parcel, as once
for a first-born child, she, who could not do a
prosaic thing, scattered a handful of fresh snow-
drops over the cardboard box to make more
artistic the baptism-robe with the stiff lace and
the insertion from the laundry-folds! She said
of her grand-aunt: "Poetry burned in her soul
higher than any flame but faith; and she was
always trying how to send home a divine truth
on the wing of a fine thought."

Lady Nairne's physician at Brussels had advised that, as far as possible, the widow, whose only son lay dying, should have some one with her—especially in her carriage on her journeys—who did not remind her of her loss. It was thus that my mother became her constant companion on the Continent for two years. Long years afterwards, when the boxes were brought out at Bonskeid for the autumn flitting south, she would recall one of the sayings of the travellers on that memorable journey, "We always get very honest at packing-time." At such times Lady Nairne's maid, Henriette, was in her element; for, like George Sand's Marie, and Michael Angelo's Urbino, and many another attendant unknown to fame, she was the faithful companion and friend for many years of her beloved mistress. Dominique, her son's servant, had fitted up a *banc à volonté* in the front part of the carriage to contain her books, work, and provisions for the day on the long drives. It was also a foot-rest.

Together, my mother and she crossed the
Stelvio and dined at the highest habitable hut
in Europe, where Lady Nairne "found the
air very invigorating." At Munich she met
Prince Albert of Saxe-Coburg with the Prince
Royal of Bavaria at quiet parties, and kept in
her writing-table the invitation to our Queen's
Coronation, with the young Sovereign's sig-
nature—a model of clear and bold writing.
She kept a book of extracts, and never read
without taking longer or shorter notes of
striking passages.

Amongst the things to be disposed of at
packing-time were articles of Lady Nairne's
own work, purchased or rather bought back
by her nieces at a bazaar for the poor. In
talking to my mother she said : " These pur-
chases remind me of the time when your dear
grandmother sent her garnets from Perth to
Ravelstone, that Aunt Keith might dispose of
them and buy a handsome folio edition of
Scott's *Commentary of the Bible* for her to

present to your grandpapa. Mr. Keith noted the jeweller's name, recovered the garnets, and kept them for your mamma." These garnets, now lying near me as I write, were given to me by my grandmother, who also told their history.

My mother could never forget the shock which she got on reaching Brussels in 1837, hoping to hear that Lord Nairne was better, to be told instead that the funeral carriages had just left the courtyard of the Rue de Louvain, nor her first sight of the beloved authoress exemplifying her own song—" Our bonnie bairn's there, John."

She once wrote : " It was a cold December night. The north wind, more dry and sifting than in Britain, was felt in the large apartment in spite of the open stove and the screen that surrounded her sofa. Lady Nairne sat at a writing-table. The green shade of the lamp concealed in a great measure the wrinkled face and blood-shot eyes ; and she looked still lovely, and much younger in her seventy-second year than one would have expected. Her cap, of Queen Mary shape, had a large white crape handkerchief thrown over it. She made the kindest and most minute inquiries about everything at home, and when the effort became too great, she gave me a book to read.

" She listened with interest to Lockhart's *Life of Sir Walter Scott*, which recalled to her the scenes and many of the personages with whom, during her residence in Edinburgh, she had been familiar. One evening, while reading aloud to her, we came upon a note discussing the authorship of ' The Land o' the Leal.' To the young reader it was somewhat like going to the cannon's mouth to read it to her, and if blushes could betray the knowledge of a secret, Lady Nairne's observant eye must have seen them.

" I never saw her allow herself to laugh heartily but once, and it was not long after our first meeting. She had been repeating some lines of which she said she had often tried to discover the author. On my insisting that his name was in a collection of poetry, she said, 'You must bring it to me next night.' She did not forget, and I told her the name of the author was 'Anonymous.   When a very little child I had got it into my mind that this was a clever man who wrote most of the pretty things we learned : not pronouncing the word properly to myself, the error had not been discovered, and the existence of 'Anon' was as firmly believed in.   To have made such a blunder before most people would have been a lasting humiliation, but not with her.   How true it is that one feels most at ease in the presence of a great mind, and never hurt or awkward!   He who has most mastered his subject will often most patiently explain its rudiments to the ignorant.

"She was kinder than ever, and said, 'Now tell me, dear Maggy, what collection of hymns do you use?'

"'*Sacred Poetry*, and Montgomery's *Christian Psalmist.*'

"'And where do you learn your hymns when at Springland?'

"'In a crooked little beech tree, just like an arm-chair, after breakfast till church time on Sundays; and other days, when there is time to go further, up at the long stone seat on the bank of Annaty Burn, where it runs into the current of the Tay, between us and the Scone grounds.'

"'The view is very fine there, is it not?'

"'We never miss going on the fine sunset evenings to see it over the Grampians; with the clouds and the broad river, and just in front of a long little island; the sky looks like a way up to heaven.'

"'What hymn did you last learn there?' she asked.

"'A cloud lay cradled near the setting sun,
    A gleam of crimson tinged its braided snow:
Long had I watched the glory moving on,
    O'er the still radiance of the lake below.'

"'Just a place to learn hymns about heaven at; they should never be learned as a task. And at Bonskeid, which is the favourite seat?'

"'Up in the west wood where you painted the house from. But last summer our governess found it dull, and we sat often on a little hill where she could see the post-runner pass, and the tourists' carriages, and the carriers' carts. She got a fright with a roe deer and an adder, and did not like the wood after.'

"'I hope they do not oblige you to write verses of your own, as some are made to do.'

"'No.'

"'And you never tried?'

"'Never.'

"'True poetry is involuntary; it will force its own way. You and I must have many talks about these wonderful men, Anonymous and Anon, who have between them caused me more delight than any authors. I must tell you a story of our youth at Gask, where the mistake of a word not only caused merriment

for us at the time, but ever since. Aunt
Harriet had got a special summons by a
messenger on horseback to Athole to go to
see Lady Lude, who was said to be so ill that
if she wished to see her in life she must come
instantly.   Aunt Harriet gave a letter, ordering
a *large chaise*, to the horseman to deliver in
Perth on his arrival there, nine miles distant,
as you know.   We all set to making preparations for her journey.   May (your grandmother) was the director, as in everything else,
and we were all seated round Aunt Harriet in
her grief, wondering how the *chaise* she had
ordered (she had written to Perth that the
biggest to be had should be sent immediately)
was so long in coming, as the journey to Blair
Athole was tedious and it was getting late.
Suddenly the door of the room opened, and
two men entered carrying an enormous *cheese !*
Aunt Harriet was always a great laugher, but
this time (owing to the tension on the nerves
caused by sorrowful preparations, parting with

us, and the illness of her sister) she was seized with an immoderate fit. Tears even ran down, the more her ludicrous mistake in spelling became plain to her. She without power to explain, the two men with the cheese on the floor between them, we gazing in utter wonder, formed a scene we could never forget. The journey was given up till next morning.'"

With that tour abroad were continually bound up memories of a dear old lady whom we all called "Cousin," Margaret Harriet Steuart, who was the daughter of Mrs. Steuart of Dalguise—Lady Nairne's sister Amelia. In a green old age her store of memories is very rich.

When the writer was a child, Miss Steuart was living at Wynberg, Cape of Good Hope, with her brother the Chief Justice of the colony. Our mother used to dictate to us letters to the distant cousin, and now she alone is left of the group who spent that time together. She was a reverent observer of

Lady Nairne's times of deep sorrow, and saw
how the energy of the mountain torrent fell into
the deep lake of later life—not to expend itself
in selfish idleness, but in self-forgetfulness, let-
ting the surface be frozen over to bear up com-
panions in sorrow who would else have sunk.

As much speaking tired her, we asked her to
put down on paper her memories of her aunt,
Lady Nairne ; and we received, in the form of
a letter, this precious piece of chronology.   It
is written by a hand that was learning to hold
a pencil when the century began, and carries
into its closing years much of the fineness of
work and deftness of touch, so hard to attain
in the bustle of our railway age.   At ninety-
seven she paints, plays and embroiders ; and
has lately sent a little work through the press.
She remembers Trafalgar and Waterloo, has
entertained Sir Walter Scott with her music,
and tells how in the daytime Miss Scott and
she would shut the shutters that they might
tell one another ghost stories in the dark.

When all the rage is for old furniture, old pictures, old wine, here is a manuscript not with yellow, mouldy markings, but precious; it is rare to get chronology from so old a living memory, reckonings from such an old ledger. She corroborates the accounts of Lady Nairne's wish for secrecy, and how she wrote under the title of Mrs. Bogan of Bogan for the *Scottish Minstrel*. She acts the part of critic too, wondering how anyone could say " The Land o' the Leal" was composed in old age, when it was written in Lady Nairne's prime. But we leave her to tell her own story.

" My earliest recollections of my Aunt Nairne are of spending a winter with her at Montrose, when I was about seven years old. She was very fond of children; and in the evenings my eldest brother John and I were always allowed by her to cut out paper, paste, paint, or make any mess we pleased; and we were much annoyed when nurse came and proclaimed that it was bedtime! Then my

dear mother and I paid a short visit to her
at Portobello. It was then that they made the
purchase of Caroline Cottage, now, I am told,
called Nairne Lodge. My next recollection is
a very sad one—soon after my mother's death.
This time I went with my Aunt Margaret
Oliphant, afterwards Mrs Keith of Dunnottar.
Aunt Nairne asked if I remembered with whom
I had come before! The answer was *tears*.

"Major Nairne, as well as his lady, was
always extremely kind to me. She called me
'Quiet Maggy,' for I was not loquacious in
those days, being rather shy. In June 1808,
my Cousin William was born in Hope Street,
Edinburgh, my aunt and I being then in the
house. The next winter was spent by the
Nairnes at 43 Queen Street, Edinburgh, and
I lived with them for two years, going daily to
school. In July 1813, I accompanied Major
and Lady Nairne in a cutter bound for the
Shetland Isles. To them I went; but poor
Aunt Nairne was so ill at sea that we had to

lay to at Peterhead whilst she and her boy were put ashore, and they both went to St. Andrews by land, where they joined your great-grandmother, my Aunt Stewart of Bonskeid.

"My next visit to Aunt Nairne was at Holyrood House, where her husband had the royal apartments for some years, until His Majesty George IV. thought fit to show himself in Scotland. It was a very pleasant dwelling. The side of the square was gloomy, but the windows of the living rooms all looked to the Park and Arthur's Seat. The chambers were of a very large size, except two smaller ones which were divided off by high screens. These were hung with very fine old tapestry, whereon were depicted immense human forms with the heads of toads. One of these chambers was my bedroom when I visited the Palace, and I confess to very eerie sensations as I looked at them at night. One anteroom was so very spacious that it was divided off into several, and allotted to the servants. The whole royal apartments were done up and beautified for the King; and to the very great amusement of my young cousin, the throne was placed exactly where the cook's bed had stood! In 1830 Lord Nairne, whose forfeited title had been restored, died at Caroline Cottage.

"In 1834 we all went to Italy and spent the greater part of the winter at Rome. Aunt Nairne went sometimes to the wonderful galleries, and I think she once ascended the outside of St. Peter's to see the village on the roof. Mrs. Keith and I came home in October 1835, but we joined in the autumn of the following year at Berlin, and there my poor cousin caught the cold which proved fatal in December 1837.

"I have found several mistakes in written memoirs of my aunt. Their son was not delicate, neither was it on account of his health that he and his mother went abroad. The cold caught at Berlin was the beginning of his illness.

"I was with her later on at Pau and Eaux

3

Chaudes.   I remember staying in a very
dilapidated chateau, where the servants were
so frightened by mysterious noises that we

LORD NAIRNE BEFORE HIS RESTORATION

had to leave sooner than we intended.   The
society in these out-of-the-way places is very
primitive, the ladies seldom wearing bonnets.

One nice, elderly dame had a very lively
recollection of the Peninsular War, and told
me that when the troops were all about, they

CAROLINE BARONESS NAIRNE
née OLIPHANT OF GASK

applied to the British for protection, as they
placed more confidence in them than in their
own soldiers. The winter that we spent at

Pau was the time of the Civil War in Spain, and the defeated Carlists came to Pau and had small pensions from the French. After this we were in the Pyrenees again, at Biarritz and Paris. It was to that city, in the spring of 1843, that James Oliphant of Gask came and took my aunt home to Gask, as you know, to die."

With this quaint piece of writing, came the three miniatures, of which we reproduce photographs. On the back of each was written the name of the person—" Caroline, Baroness Nairne, née Oliphant of Gask "; " Lord Nairne, before his restoration"; "William Murray, last Lord Nairne, died 1837, aged 29."

Our last summer's visit to Gask made this document and all our previous information glow with a new interest. In and out through that avenue gate had Neil Gow passed with his fiddle to charm the youthful occupants, and set one of the company composing lines to sing to his catching airs. Above one of her

songs. "Caller Herrin'," is printed, "Air by
Neil Gow." Since the above was written,
Madame Antoinette Sterling has told us how

WILLIAM MURRAY
last LORD NAIRNE

she met lately the great-grandson of Neil
Gow in Hobart, Tasmania. He spoke of his
ancestor having composed the tune of "Caller

Herrin'!" Many of the airs to which Burns
wrote songs had been of the old fiddler's
composition, and she was shown a drawing
of Neil Gow fiddling to Burns sitting on a
bench, with Mrs. Burns sitting on a chair at the
end of the bench. Both Madame Antoinette
Sterling's friend and his son inherit the musical
gifts of the family.

When a friend thought Lady Nairne was
writing love-letters the letters were poems. If
the ruin of the "Auld House" could speak,
it would tell us how the cause of its being
pulled down was the rats eating into the
cradle of the baby, and how, when the Bible
was removed in state from the old house to
the new, the door gave way on its hinges!
My mother used to tell how Lady Nairne
was born into a nursery where two others
besides herself had been named for Prince
Charles Edward—Charles, Charlotte, Caroline;
and how these children prayed from prayer-
books on which the names of the exiled family

were pasted over those of the reigning house. And then, how the beautiful Caroline had learned her lessons under the tuition of the old Abbé Maitland, a Non-conformist clergyman, and become an adept at all she tried. To Gask she returned to die. In a cool ante-room of the new house, in her last days, she might still be found taking her invalid's walk. There she was, passing and repassing the bust of her darling son, and stopping as often to gaze on it, then replacing the white handkerchief that covered it to keep it pure. Yet there was gladness in the retrospect, for of him she wrote: "I have not a single regret about William's upbringing. He was trained for the Kingdom, whither he has gone." The thoughts in her last song, written in 1842, would be uppermost as she looked back on her long pilgrimage:

"Would you be young again?
So would not I—
One tear to memory giv'n,
Onward I'd hie.

Life's dark flood forded o'er,
All but at rest on shore,
Say, would you plunge once more,
  With home so nigh?

Where are they gone, of yore
  My best delight?
Dear and more dear, tho' now
  Hidden from sight.
Where they rejoice to be,
There is the land for me ;
Fly time, fly speedily ;
  Come life and light !"

On long winter evenings in our town house in the Square, the sight of the oil painting, by Sir John Watson Gordon, of Lady Nairne and her son over the mantelpiece (of which we reproduce a photograph in our frontispiece), would recall to our mother her second visit to Brussels, when the door was slammed in her face by new occupants, and the visit, after fifteen years to Lord Nairne's grave, with the stone on which she had seen the inscription carved—

"WILLIAM, LORD NAIRNE, Aged 29
Blessed are the Dead which die in the Lord."

Here are the lines found in Lady Nairne's desk after her death, which bear on this season of sorrow—

"Go, call for the mourners, and raise the lament,
  Let the tresses be torn, and the garments be rent;
  But weep not for him who is gone to his rest,
  Nor mourn for the ransom'd, nor wail for the blest.
  Their sun is not set, but is risen on high,
  Nor long in corruption their bodies shall lie.
  Then let not the tide of thy griefs overflow,
  Nor the music of heaven be discord below—
  Rather, loud be the song, and triumphant the chord,
  Let us joy for THE DEAD WHO HAVE DIED IN THE LORD

  Go, call for the mourners, and raise the lament,
  Let the tresses be torn, and the garments be rent;
  But give to the living thy passion of tears,
  Who walk in this valley of sadness and fears—
  Who are pressed by the combat, in darkness are lost.
  By the tempest are beat, on the billows are tost.
  Oh, weep not for them who shall sorrow no more,
  Whose warfare is ended, whose combat is o'er—
  Let the song be exalted, triumphant the chord,
  And rejoice for THE DEAD WHO HAVE DIED IN THE LORD.

In turning over some papers, we came upon the copy of a poem in Lady Nairne's own writing, where a verse is transposed in different

order from the way the poem stands in her
songs. The paper is brown and mouldy, and
the writing hasty. It looks like a first sketch
of the published one called "Songs of my
Native Land." To my mother, who had been
teaching a class in the Tower at Springland,
and who had told her of a new hymn which the
children had been learning to sing, she said,
"Repeat it." "There is a Happy Land"
was the hymn. She listened attentively to the
close, and said—"It is pretty, very sweet,
but might be clearer." It looks as if she
had dashed off this "Parody," as she calls it
according to the custom of the time, immediately after. Later, on hearing the tune
or seeing the hymn in print, she found that
she had not caught the metre. In producing
a second copy of her poem, she at the same
time wrote a new verse, and transposed the
second and third stanzas.

Here is the original sketch, title and all, as
it appears in the MS.—

"PARODY OF 'I'M COME FROM A HAPPY LAND.'[1]

" I'm bound for a happy land,
　Where care is unknown ;
I am bound for a happy land,
　Where love reigns alone.
Come, come, and fly with me,
Love's banquet waits for thee,
Joy, joy, and ecstasy, for evermore.

Weary pilgrims there have rest,
　Their wanderings o'er ;
There the slave, no more oppressed,
　Hails Freedom's shore.
Sin will there no more deface ;
Sickness, pain, and sorrow cease,
Ending in eternal peace
　And songs of joy.

Strains of my native land
　That thrill the soul,
Pouring the magic of your self-control.
Oft has your minstrelsy
Soothed the pang of misery,
Winging swift thought away,
　To realms on high.

---

[1] Lady Nairne, having heard the hymn only once repeated,
evidently mistook its title, and thought it was " I'm Come from
a Happy Land," instead of " There is a Happy Land."

> There, where the seraphs sing
> In cloudless day ;
> There, where their higher praise
> The ransomed pay—
> Hymns of the happy land,
> Chanted by the heavenly band,
> Who, who can understand
> How sweet ye be !"

The final form, in which the song was presented to the world, has quite a different turn given to it. It is headed, " Songs of my Native Land."

> "Songs of my native land,
>   To me how dear !
> Songs of my infancy,
>   Sweet to mine ear !
> Entwined with my youthful days,
> Wi' the bonny banks and braes,
> Where the winding burnie strays
>   Murmuring near.
>
> Strains of my native land
>   That thrill the soul,
> Pouring the magic of
>   Your self-control !
> Often has your minstrelsy
> Soothed the pang of misery,
> Winging rapid thought away
>   To realms on high.

Weary pilgrims *there* have rest,
  Their wand'rings o'er ;
There the slave, no more oppressed,
  Hails Freedom's shore.
Sin shall there no more deface,
Sickness, pain, and sorrow cease,
Ending in eternal peace,
  And songs of joy !

There, where the seraphs sing
  In cloudless day, –
There, where the higher praise
  The ransom'd pay.
Soft strains of the happy land,
Chanted by the heavenly band,
Who can fully understand
  How sweet ye be !"

As we look on her writing, we wonder why
the veil of secrecy was so closely drawn, and
that her poetry did not rend it asunder. But
her will was determined. Only a very few
besides my mother and grandmother knew
who wrote the songs.

From the friends who looked in of an
evening on the Continent, as was then the
custom, she kept her secret even to the end.
For example, when she was asked to write in

an album, and someone looked eagerly to see
what she had written, thinking that now the
poet would have revealed herself, the lines set
down were not her own but Montgomery's.
It had been the same with the visitors
whom she met at Ravelstone, near Edinburgh.
Here, as recorded by Dr. Rogers in his
Life and Songs of the Baroness Nairne, guests
were wont to arrive early each Saturday.
After lunching on hotch-potch, cocky-leeky, and
haggis, they took dessert out of doors, under
the old forest trees. After tea, music and
singing began. A young lady sang a ballad,
but could not finish all the verses. A visitor
told her to go to the end of the room where
she would find a lady who would finish the
song. It was Lady Nairne. They became
staunch friends, and to her Lady Nairne con-
fided, some years after, that she had penned
"The Land o' the Leal," adding, with a smile,
"I have not even told Nairne, lest he blab."
It was said that her husband's recovery of the

I've heard the lilting
At our ewes milking
Lasses a lilting before break of day
But now there's a moaning
On ilka green loaning
Since the flowers of the forest are a wed away

At bughts in the gloaming
Nae blythe lads are roaming
'Mang stacks in the byres at high to bling
Nae laughing nae gabbin but sighing & sabbing
Ilk ane lifts her leglin & hies her away

O dool for the order
Sent our lads to the border
The English for ance by guile got the day
The flowers of the forest that aye shone the foremost
The pride of our land lies cauld in the clay
We'll hear nae mair lilting
At our ewes milking
The women & bairns are dowy & wae
Ilk ane sits dreary
Lamenting her dearie
Since our brave foresters are a wed away.

As some may like to look at her writing, we give a reduced facsimile reproduction of a fragment found among her papers. The lines consist of four verses of Jean Elliot's *Flowers of the Forest*, slightly modified.

peerage was owing to her song, " The Attainted
Scottish Nobles," being sung in the presence of
George IV., and Sir Walter Scott brought the
petition before His Majesty.

The young lady mentioned above who sang
the ballad was, in her old age, a friend of
our childhood, Miss Helen Walker of Dalry.
She used to come at meal-times to talk over
various matters with my mother, and it amused
us as children very much to see her slip cookies
and scones and fruit off the table and carry
them away in a black bag to give to the
cabmen and her poorer friends. In one of
Lady Nairne's letters to her we find her saying,
" I had been told of a musical person rather in
distress, and I had resolved—as soon as I could
secretly enough—to send the few words I had
thought of for old airs, to be published as a
mere mite of charity. I knew *novelty* and
single sheets have attractions."

When the Revolution and its horrors were
brewing in France, when the War of Indepen-

4

dence was finished in America, there was
born, almost within a decade, three singers in
Scotland—"Land of the Mountain and the
Flood!"—who loved to celebrate their native
land in song. They who wrote of "Mine own
Romantic Town," "Ye Banks and Braes o'
Bonnie Doon," and "Oh, the Auld House,
the Auld House," were all children about the
same time, drinking in the same native air.
Burns was seven years Lady Nairne's senior;
and Scott and she by a few hours missed
having the same birthday, only Scott came
five years later on the scene.

Thus running almost parallel with her life,
on either side was a chain of mountains of
Alpine grandeur, with such peaks rearing their
heads as "Waverley," "Heart of Midlothian,"
and "Redgauntlet"; and opposite, if not so
defined against the sky, yet with outlines of
the boldest, there was another range, but only
for a time did they appear, as Burns died
early. We might compare his songs to grassy

rounded hills, some wooded to the top, so restful, grateful, and comforting — the "Cottar's Saturday Night," the "Banks and Braes," and anon the bolder form of " Scots wha hae."

In between these flowed our brook, with an individuality all its own. Constantly hearing from her father the old Jacobite stories, and seeing the relics arrive at Gask from the Prince, she could not help the sentiments creating and colouring her songs. Our stream ran on through "The Ploughman," "He's a terrible man, John Tod, John Tod," "Laird o' Cockpen," and other humorous poems.

Our streamlet now and then wandered out of sight altogether for a time, then broke forth in "The Rowan Tree," "Bonnie ran the Burnie," and in that exquisite fisher song "Caller Herrin'," with the smell of the sea in every line.

Again, the strain bursts forth in ripples and rapids and rushing waterfalls, " Wi' a Hundred Pipers an' a', an' a'," and "Charlie is my

Darling,"—echoes as they doubtless are of the notes of Neil Gow's fiddle. Then the deep-flowing, still sadness of the stream gave later on "The Auld House," and "The Land o' the Leal." In the decade between 1820 and 1830, a breath had surely blown from the range above, when she began the poem entitled, "Jeanie Deans."

> "St. Leonard's hill was lightsome land
>   Where gowan'd grass was growin',
> For man and beast were food and rest
>   And milk and honey flowin'."

It was probably when she left Caroline Cottage in 1830, for a southern climate, that she wrote her "Farewell to Edinburgh," in which she specially mentions Sir Walter.

> "Fareweel, Edinburgh, your sons o' genius fine,
>   That send your name on wings o' fame beyond the burnin'
>   line ;
>   A name that's stood maist since the flood, and just when
>   it's forgot,
>   Your bard will be forgotten too, your ain Sir Walter Scott."

Then, after a period of great suffering we
hear her voice again in her seventy-sixth year
in the sweet, sad strains of "Would You be
Young Again," in which our streamlet, ere
it falls into the sea, recalls the music of its
mountain source.   Once the spring of poetry
comes welling up, many influences swell the
volume of the stream.   Emotions trouble it,
fine scenery is reflected in it, for nature will
never let it lack inviting subjects.   But the
spring must be there, we cannot manufacture
it at will.

Burns sought to purify what went before his
time, and to our singer's soul Burns himself
needed purifying.   The woman was supplying
the delicacy and tenderness of feeling for
which the greater bard would have been the
first to thank her.

So down through our ages will go the influence of song, binding together families and
nations, years and centuries.   One night on
the banks of the Potomac, as the Confederate

and the Union troops lay opposite to each
other, the Union bands played "The Star-
Spangled Banner," "Hail Columbia," and other
Union songs, and the Confederates in contest
played "Dixie," "The Bonnie Blue Flag," and
other songs so dear to them. It seemed for a
while that each would play the other down.
By and by one band struck up "Home, sweet
Home," and the contest was at an end, the
vast multitudes on both sides of the river took
up the words, and sang in unison,

"There's no place like home."

We know not what advances music and song
may make. This we know, that the *power*
will go down the centuries. In an audience a
speaker cannot satisfy all his listeners; some
are above his level, some below. But join in
a song and differences cease. Men may differ
as to tactics of war, but their voices blend in
the battle-cry. Like a new reaping machine,
it binds as it cuts. "Let who will, write the
history of a country, give me its songs."

It is said that the beautiful air, " Hey Tuttie Taitie," to which "The Land o' the Leal" is sung, was played on the field of Bannockburn. It can ring out martial strains as in " Scots wha hae," or plaintive notes as in " The Land o' the Leal," according to the time it is played in. Professor Masson has said of Lady Nairne's songs : " There is a real *moral* worth in them all, and all that genuine characteristic of a song which consists of an inner *tune* preceding and inspiring the words, and coiling the words as it were out of the heart along with it." Another merit of these songs is their word-painting, for their sweet music seems to grow on us each time we see a rowan tree, meet a Newhaven fishwife, wander by a bonnie burn, hear a Highland piper, visit an old ruin, or watch the melting snow ; and added years only in- crease and deepen our love of these *Lays of Strathcarn.*

In an evening gathering all are not alike musical, and unless the Italian and German words are sung by one of their own nationality, even for practised ears it is often difficult to hear, and when heard they may not be understood. With an indifferent look of worked-up interest the name of the composer is asked. When the music is over there is often a sense of relief, and conversation bursts out with a kind of feeling of revenge. But when a Scotch song or English ballad is sung, and sung well, friends meet on common ground, and unconsciously they are at once drawn nearer to each other.

At sixteen, Lady Nairne wrote : " I do think fine music engrosses all the senses, and leaves not one faculty of the mind unemployed." And all through life, though the course of her song may have been devious, the aim was straight. When her footman returned with the yellow-covered book which was selling at the fair, and she found many unsuitable words in the songs, Caroline went home and wrote a new version of the " Ploughman," to be

sung at a dinner of the Gask tenantry.   In
youth she had been dauntless.   The word
"impossible" did not exist in her vocabulary.
When at a ball in a watering-place the ladies
were found too few for a dance, she drove
home, awoke a friend at midnight, and stood in
waiting till the sleeper was equipped to follow
her to the ballroom.

As she wrote in secrecy, and only before
her death allowed her songs to be collected,
but without her name, so her gifts were in
secret too.   After her death, Dr. Chalmers
said that he might now say that the anonymous donor of £300 to his work in the
West Port, Edinburgh, was from a lady of
another communion, Lady Nairne of Perthshire, but he did not know to add, authoress
of "The Land o' the Leal."

The poet was a painter too.   The artist
must have his surroundings in harmony with
himself, and at all costs will he remove the
objects that jar, and retain only such as rest

and stimulate. The sweet singer, holding
communion with nature, not only had sung
of "The Rowan Tree," but had painted fruit
trees at different stages of growth, which are
treasured at Gask. The picture of Gask in
the *Lays from Strathearn*, is from her pencil;
and when her health permitted, her sketch-
book was only laid down when the weather
grew too cold. At Caroline Cottage she had
her studio where she painted; and in her room
at Enniskerry, where the whole of the wall
was stained with damp, like Leonardo da Vinci
on the walls of the Milan refectory, she
sketched with common black lead the landscape
near. But it was not merely for her own
enjoyment that she painted; for she says, " I
pay myself for my work, which fills my purse
best when I consider the time occupied rather
than the merit of the performances. This re-
minds me of your query as to the best mode
of appropriating charity cash; my own opinion
has always been that devoting a proportion is

the best way." She gave freely what she had
worked to give. Henriette was the bearer to
my mother of old silver forks and spoons with
the crest, of which the value, after their being
melted, was to go to Dr. Chalmers for the
Sustentation Fund of the Free Church.

Mr. Kington Oliphant, the present accom-
plished Laird of Gask, tells in his history of
his Jacobite predecessors how in 1868 he saw
Henriette Vouaillat at Geneva. "After listen-
ing to a long catalogue of the virtues of one
who had been dead a score of years, I asked
in French, 'But had your mistress no faults?
You are describing a perfect character.' 'Sir,'
said the old Genevese, 'My mistress came as
near to an angel as the weakness of human
nature would allow; the only thing amiss I
could see in her was that she disliked my
marrying or otherwise leaving her.'"

The end was drawing near, and she put all
in order. It was October in the country. In

our city gardens and squares the leaves soon look sickly and soiled, and quickly fall. Not so in the fresh country surroundings. In a fine gleam on Saturday, 25th October, Lady Nairne was wheeled in her chair through the long familiar grounds of Gask. She stopped at the door of the little chapel, which she had helped to build, on the site of the old parish church. As they were leaving, she said to my grandmother, "The place will soon be ready for me." On returning to the house, she complained of breathlessness, and next day had lost all power of speech. Outside, the autumn tints were colouring the landscape, - not only yellow, green and brown, but crimson. Frost was in the air. Nature was decaying, the days were shortening, the year was dying. The songstress had long lain on the border-land, and had taken quick flights, and brought messages back from the other shore. She had loved the imagery of the *Pilgrim's Progress,* and said, " Fearful got safely into the Celestial

City, but he had a weary pilgrimage; I would rather go with Faithful." The Sabbath dawned; the workmen rested; nature rested too. Our dove returned not. No more olive leaves of promise were needed. She had found rest in the "Land o' the Leal."

One of Lady Nairne's maxims was: "Religion is a walking and not a talking concern." She did not wish the surface only, but the whole being to be saturated. It is true both of nations and of individuals, that if we are to assist the great march forward, it will not be by singing ditties and pulling flowers by the roadside. A widow left alone, her only son gone, might be excused if she half closed the shutters of her life and sought repose. Instead, she braced herself up for unfinished tasks on the unfinished journey. We see, in the picture of herself and her son in our frontispiece, how gladly that arm encircled her child. But when he was gone, there were others needing help. Speaking of

pictures she was painting for three frames
which she happened to have, she says they
"are nearly finished; that means done with,
for finished they are not." Keynote of every
true worker before and since! For, unless
the singer is a worker, his poesy is nought;
done with it may be, finished it is not. The
strength of every true worker is his ideal.
In the block of marble, in the newly-stretched
canvas, in the unwritten score, there lie the
possibilities of what the worker and the work
may alike become. What lures him onward?
Not the fairy palaces of the golden dreams
of childhood, where the doors flew open, and
the right person walked in and the disagreeable
stepped out; where the coin came unasked to
the beggar's hand, and the reward unworked
for to the sluggard; where there was no
interruption, and consequently no struggle. It
is the ideal of what, having once in vision
gilded his own horizon, is not as yet. And
if, even after the hard ascent, it be but to find

another height beyond, who would compare the joy of toiling with the monotony of loitering in the plain beneath?

Amid the ardour of youth, the sorrow and trials of widowhood, the sting of lost motherhood, with a coronet or without it, courting no applause in her gifts as in her songs, making her own maxims and following them, she has left for us, in the closing years of this century, words that touch our hearts and tune our voices, because into the humanity of the woman was breathed the inspiration of the Divine.

MARGARET STEWART SIMPSON.

www.ingramcontent.com/pod-product-compliance
Lightning Source LLC
Chambersburg PA
CBHW021531090426
42739CB00007B/878